LONDON

THE CITY AT A GLANCE

Tower 42
Richard Seifert's 1980 skyscraper, still known
as the NatWest Tower by most locals, now
has the added draw of City Social (see p041).
25 Old Broad Street, EC2

30 St Mary Axe
The famous 'Gherkin' shape of this 180m
diamond-patterned tower, which bulges at its
midpoint, staves off street-level wind tunnels.
30 St Mary Axe, EC3

St Paul's Cathedral
Christopher Wren's landmark is being steadily
overshadowed by nearby developments.
St Paul's Churchyard, EC4, T 7246 8350

Leadenhall Building
Completed in 2014, this bold 54-storey office
tower is kingpin of the Square Mile, for now.
See p012

20 Fenchurch Street
Maligned because of its shape and an early
design flaw, the 'Walkie-Scorchie' hopes to
gain admirers with its Sky Garden.
20 Fenchurch Street, EC3

Millennium Bridge
Due to teething problems, when the rush-
hour stomp caused it to vibrate, Foster +
Partners' span is dubbed the 'wobbly bridge'.

The Shard
An entire district, London Bridge Quarter, is
being created below the city's new emblem.
See p010

Tate Modern
Bankside's contemporary art museum is
one of London's foremost success stories.
See p068

INTRODUCTION

THE CHANGING FACE OF THE URBAN SCENE

Twenty years ago, London's claim to be one of the world's greatest cities was unconvincing. Now, it is arguably *the* global city, truly multicultural and economically influential – a wellspring of both creativity and commerce. Not that there aren't problems, of course. Competition for space and the rocketing cost of living have made manifold aspects the privilege of the few and not the majority. Yet the energy and the spirit that drive the metropolis come from all quarters, and that is what makes it exceptional.

London scatters its treasures far and wide, and as new focal points crystallise all the time, its many pleasures remain diverse. The scramble to the South-East, prompted by The Shard (see p010), is turning the area into a hive of activity, and in King's Cross and Victoria, regeneration is at full speed. One glimpse at Old Street's Silicon Roundabout shows the city as a digital innovator, and the willingness of investors to back start-ups means there are more opportunities than ever to get projects and ideas off the ground.

Post-recession, there's a good-times vibe. As a destination for art and design, the capital's standing has never been higher, while the boldness and integrity of its restaurants and cafés now equal that of its great transatlantic rival, New York. The Big Smoke may not be a 24-hour playground yet, but for all its fickleness, provocations and cliques, London is a magnificent place to be. The challenge is plotting a course through it all. And that is where we come in.

ESSENTIAL INFO
FACTS, FIGURES AND USEFUL ADDRESSES

TOURIST OFFICE
St Paul's Churchyard, EC4
T 7332 1456
www.visitlondon.com

TRANSPORT
Heathrow transfer to Paddington
Trains depart regularly from 5.10am to
11.45pm. The journey takes 15 minutes
www.heathrowexpress.com
Bicycles
Bikes can be hired across central London
www.tfl.gov.uk
Car hire
Avis
T 0844 581 0147
Public transport
Tube trains run from roughly 5.30am to
12.30am, Monday to Saturday; 6.30am to
12am, Sunday. Trains will run for 24 hours
at weekends from September 2015
www.tfl.gov.uk
Taxis
Addison Lee
T 7407 9000
Travel card
A one-day zones 1-2 pass costs £9;
a seven-day zones 1-2 pass costs £31.40

EMERGENCY SERVICES
Emergencies
T 999
Late-night pharmacy
Bliss
5-6 Marble Arch, W1
T 7723 6116

EMBASSY
US Embassy
24 Grosvenor Square, W1
T 7499 9000
london.usembassy.gov

POSTAL SERVICES
Post office
The Plaza, W1
T 7636 9584
Shipping
UPS
T 0845 161 0016

BOOKS
**London's Contemporary Architecture:
An Explorer's Guide** by Ken Allinson and
Victoria Thornton (Routledge)
Unseen London by Peter Dazeley and
Mark Daly (Frances Lincoln)

WEBSITES
Architecture
www.architecture.com
www.newlondonarchitecture.org
Newspaper
www.standard.co.uk

EVENTS
Frieze Art Fair
www.friezelondon.com
London Design Festival
www.londondesignfestival.com
Open House London
www.londonopenhouse.org

COST OF LIVING
**Taxi from Heathrow Airport
to city centre**
£60
Cappuccino
£2.80
Packet of cigarettes
£9
Daily newspaper
£1.60
Bottle of champagne
£70

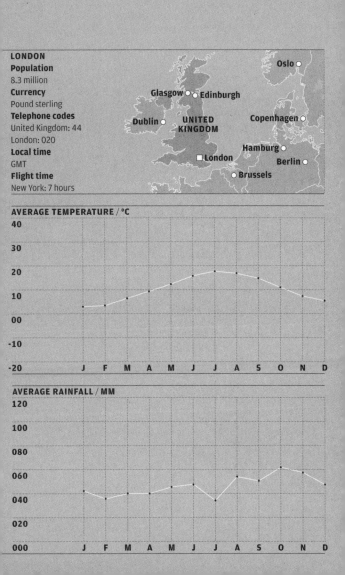

LONDON
Population
8.3 million
Currency
Pound sterling
Telephone codes
United Kingdom: 44
London: 020
Local time
GMT
Flight time
New York: 7 hours

Oslo
Glasgow ○○ Edinburgh
Copenhagen ○
Dublin ○ **UNITED KINGDOM**
Hamburg ○
Berlin ○
□ London
○ Brussels

AVERAGE TEMPERATURE / °C

40
30
20
10
00
-10
-20
J F M A M J J A S O N D

AVERAGE RAINFALL / MM

120
100
080
060
040
020
000
J F M A M J J A S O N D

NEIGHBOURHOODS
THE AREAS YOU NEED TO KNOW AND WHY

To help you navigate the city, we've chosen the most interesting districts (see below and the map inside the back cover) and colour-coded our featured venues, according to their location; those venues that are outside these areas are not coloured.

CENTRAL
The West End is the centre of the modern city, and feels more vibrant than in recent years. Mayfair is a gallery hot zone (see p056) and, on the borders of Bloomsbury, Holborn's renaissance is evidenced by new hotels such as Rosewood (see p019). As a nocturnal playground, Soho has won back some kudos from the East.

NORTH
Traditionally, the hills of North London have had a bohemian air, and they boast some of the finest modernist buildings in the capital (see p072). Next to chichi Primrose Hill, Camden gets clogged with tourists, while King's Cross is undergoing a massive urban overhaul (see p074).

THE CITY
A close-knit mesh of medieval streets, Victorian pubs and a growing stockpile of 21st-century towers (see p012), the financial centre of the capital was once deserted at night, but that's beginning to change thanks to the likes of Jason Atherton's City Social (see p041).

SOUTH-WEST
Purest posh, this district has some of the most expensive property on the planet. You can hardly move for lords, ladies, oil millionaires and Russian oligarchs. It's also home to one of London's finest museums, the V&A (see p028), and an increasing number of decent restaurants (see p032).

WEST
Notting Hill can feel like a fantasy land, complete with stucco townhouses, cute boutiques and the picturesque Portobello market, and many visitors believe they've found an urban idyll. Dining highlights include The Ledbury (127 Ledbury Road, W11, T 7792 9090), and Dock Kitchen (see p051), near Trellick Tower (see p015).

WESTMINSTER
Britain's administrative heart, once the seat of a global empire, is the country's ancient and whirring engine room, and Victoria (see p030) is a district on the up. After a tour of Tate Britain (Millbank, SW1, T 7887 8888), take a river boat over to Bankside to survey it all from the Thames.

EAST
Over the past decade, this district has dragged the epicentre of cool eastwards. Shoreditch is still a stomping ground, and has good design shops (see p080), but the trendsetters have long decamped to Hackney and Dalston. Bethnal Green (see p034) is in the midst of gentrification.

SOUTH-EAST
Tate Modern (see p068) is the significant attraction here, although it's no longer the main reason to venture south of the river. Bermondsey (see p071) has developed into a destination in its own right, and is quickly filling up with eateries and art galleries, while Peckham has a scene all of its own.

LANDMARKS
THE SHAPE OF THE CITY SKYLINE

Cluttered with cranes and as fluid as the Thames, London's skyline has undergone radical change in the past decade. It's difficult to imagine now, but it was once low rise. Until the 1960s, the height of new buildings was prescribed, not by some masterplan, but by how high a fireman's ladder could reach. Inevitably, this changed. The BT Tower (see p014), thrusting upwards like a *2001: A Space Odyssey* film set *avant la lettre*, seemed to be a manifestation of a better future. Then it became a race for the sky, with the big players acquiring jocular nicknames. In the noughties, Foster + Partners' 'Gherkin' (30 St Mary Axe) took on iconic status, although its role as the City's totemic tower has been taken by Rogers Stirk Harbour + Partners' 'Cheesegrater' (see p012). Nearby, Rafael Viñoly's 20 Fenchurch Street, dubbed the 'Walkie-Talkie', or 'Fryscraper', after sunlight bouncing off its facade melted a car below, muscles into view. Surpassing them all, at almost 310m, Renzo Piano's The Shard (overleaf) has become the capital's defining landmark. Derided by some, it's impossible to ignore and hard to resist.

In West London, the looming Trellick Tower (see p015) was equally controversial in its time (JG Ballard allegedly based his novel *High-Rise*, in which tenants begin floor-on-floor warfare, on this block). Yet architect Ernö Goldfinger's brutalist triumph has since become a cult item, and is now highly desirable real estate. *For full addresses, see Resources.*

The Shard

Soaring over the diminutive red brick of
Borough, the tallest tower in Western
Europe is an astonishing spectacle that
appears in your line of sight from even
the most unexpected corners of London.
Credit to Arup, it's also a remarkable feat
of engineering. It has 95 storeys, 44 lifts
travelling at 6m per second, and houses
a Shangri-La hotel, restaurants, offices
penthouses and an observation deck.
It's not without its critics. It interrupts
many supposedly protected views and
is a giant glass tower when giant glass
towers have a bad rap (although its triple
glazing and blind system reduce cooling
costs). Dubai horror or not, it has an
ambition that most locals have come
to admire, the facade creating stunning
effects on the dullest of London days.
32 London Bridge Street, SE1,
www.the-shard.com

Leadenhall Building

The UK's tallest office tower is a postscript to its neighbour, the 1986 Lloyd's Building. When Richard Rogers designed the latter, now Grade-I listed, he injected visual and structural daring into the City with a high-tech style the architect had explored in the 1977 Centre Pompidou in Paris. RSH+P's Leadenhall is a more refined but similarly spirited structure. At 224.5m, it slices past Norman Foster's Gherkin (see p009) and Richard Seifert's Tower 42, its 18,000-tonne steel frame revealed through the glass skin. To protect views to St Paul's, the principal facade leans back by 10 degrees, which earnt the building its 'Cheesegrater' nickname. Hoisted 28m on giant struts, it ascends over a public plaza intended to give some space back to the dense City. *122 Leadenhall Street, EC3, T 7220 8960, www.theleadenhallbuilding.com*

Centre Point

Richard Seifert's influence on the London cityscape is unmatched (cast an eye over his 1962 Space House at 1 Kemble Street, WC2), but not always in a good way. When this office high-rise was unveiled in 1966, it was the tallest building in the capital. Yet it was also, famously, one of the most underutilised. The developer, Harry Hyams, wanted to rent it to a single tenant and, as a result, it stood empty for many years.

Schemes to turn it into housing have been mooted over the decades, but it would appear that its legacy will be as a pointer to shoppers on Oxford Street, and to the power of the property magnate's greed. On the top floors, the Paramount restaurant (T 7420 2900) and Tom Dixon-designed Zinc bar both provide some of the most dramatic panoramas in town.
101-103 New Oxford Street, WC1

BT Tower

Unusually for an instantly recognisable landmark, the BT Tower (formerly known as the Post Office Tower) did not appear on any maps during the first 30 years of its existence. As a microwave relay station for the national phone company – fabulously exotic technology for the time – it was an unlikely inclusion in the Official Secrets Act, and surely the only one with a revolving restaurant on top. But then, ever since it was officially opened in 1966 by a noted left-wing politician (Tony Benn) and the owner of a chain of holiday camps (Billy Butlin), the structure has always been a mix of contradictions. The restaurant was bombed by the IRA in 1971 and was closed in 1980, although occasionally it's used for corporate events. As a telecoms tower, the building is still in operation.
60 Cleveland Street, W1

Trellick Tower

Ernö Goldfinger's high-rise looms over the stuccoed townhouses and chichi eateries of Ladbroke Grove – a last blast of top-quality brutalism in the UK. The architect started work on the 31-storey structure in 1969 and it was completed in 1972. The look is of a monumental concrete slab with add-ons. It is defined by a separate service tower connected to the 'living units' in the main building by concealed walkways every third floor, and the rather menacing cantilevered boiler house that perches on top like a ship's bridge. The apartments themselves are huge, for social housing, and have large balconies. Goldfinger was also a talented furniture designer and took obsessive care of the details, from the cedar cladding to double-glazed windows that spin round for ease of cleaning.

5 Golborne Road, W10

HOTELS

WHERE TO STAY AND WHICH ROOMS TO BOOK

In The Savoy (Strand, WC2, T 7836 4343), Claridge's (Brook Street, W1, T 7629 8860) and The Dorchester (Park Lane, W1, T 7629 8888), London has some of the most famous hotels in the world, all grand ballrooms and liveried doormen. Recently, a clutch of newcomers has shaken up the scene, reinvigorating the options in key parts of town. Ian Schrager has returned to Fitzrovia, where he launched the Sanderson in 2000, to open The Edition (see p021), and up the road in Holborn, Rosewood (see p018) is a standout renovation of the 1914 Pearl Assurance Building. Minutes away, and a sign of this area's rejuvenation, Ennismore and Soho House have teamed up for The Hoxton Holborn (199-206 High Holborn, WC1, T 7661 3000), whose lobby has become a central meet-work point. Restaurateurs Chris Corbin and Jeremy King have joined the fray too, with The Beaumont (see p023), while Marylebone has been given a boost by André Balazs' Chiltern Firehouse (1 Chiltern Street, W1, T 7073 7653) and a Zetter Townhouse (28-30 Seymour Street, W1, T 7324 4567).

To the east, the Ace (opposite) is holding fast as a local gathering place, while Bethnal Green's Town Hall Hotel (Patriot Square, E2, T 7871 0460) is a perfectly judged midcentury fantasy. For those on a budget, Citizen M (20 Lavington Street, SE1, T 3519 1680) in Bankside (and Holborn from 2015) and Qbic (42 Adler Street, E1, T 3021 3300) benefit from good design and convenient locations. *For full addresses and room rates, see Resources.*

Ace Hotel

Since it arrived in 2013, the Ace, or more specifically its lobby/lounge (above), has become the de rigueur workspace for the Shoreditch set, which gives the hotel a palpable buzz. Beyond its long, communal table by Benchmark, Universal Design Studio's interiors incorporate APC quilts, rugs by Rachel Scott (see p083), Revo radios and Farmers toiletries. Of the 258 rooms, the deluxe options pull off the hip apartment feel that the Ace chain has so perfected, and the suites boast terraces overlooking Shoreditch High Street. Guests and locals hang out over coffee from the Bulldog Edition café, get a vitamin injection at Lovage juice bar, or a more substantial bite at Hoi Polloi (T 8880 6100). Basement club Miranda provides the nightlife.
100 Shoreditch High Street, E1,
T 7613 9800, www.acehotel.com/london

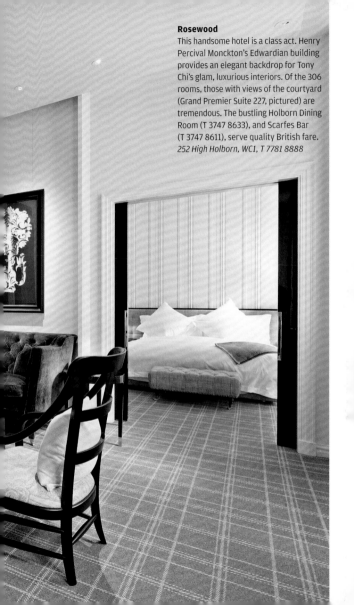

Rosewood

This handsome hotel is a class act. Henry Percival Monckton's Edwardian building provides an elegant backdrop for Tony Chi's glam, luxurious interiors. Of the 306 rooms, those with views of the courtyard (Grand Premier Suite 227, pictured) are tremendous. The bustling Holborn Dining Room (T 3747 8633), and Scarfes Bar (T 3747 8611), serve quality British fare.
252 High Holborn, WC1, T 7781 8888

Ham Yard Hotel

Tim and Kit Kemp's formula may not be to everyone's taste, but it is successful. Of the Firmdale group's eight hotels in the city, Ham Yard is the most ambitious. Decorated in Kit Kemp's amped-up, off-kilter country-house style, it's cleverly situated steps from Piccadilly Circus and fronted by Tony Cragg's sculpture *Group*. The interiors are packed with one-offs, either created by Kit (fabrics and wallpaper), or selected by her, such as the Indian tapestry in the Library (above) and Gareth Devonald Smith's bespoke light in the lobby. Firmdale excels at comfort, and the 91 rooms are snug, cheery retreats from the grit of Soho. The restaurant/bar has had mixed reviews since the 2014 opening, but the roof garden is a lovely spot for a tipple.
1 Ham Yard, W1, T 3642 2000,
www.firmdalehotels.com

The Edition

Ian Schrager's hospitality chic is the lure of the Edition brand, and in the 2013 London outpost, the slick service and sceney public spaces that he excels at are all in place. The appeal has a lot to do with the building itself, a remodelling of the 1904 Berners Hotel. In the lofty lobby, which is lined with Christian Liaigre furniture, you can't help but ogle the restored stucco and Ingo Maurer installation overhead, and Jason Atherton's Berners Tavern (T 7908 7979) is a dazzler of a dining room. There's also a lobby bar and reservation-only Punch Room. Schrager collaborated with Yabu Pushelberg on the 173 rooms (Loft, above), which are understated but stylish, and done out in dark walnut or light oak. Ask for one with plenty of natural light. *10 Berners Street, W1, T 7781 0000, www.editionhotels.com*

Mondrian

In 1978, American architect Warren Platner gave London one of its most distinctive office buildings, for the Sea Containers shipping company. Now Tom Dixon's Design Research Studio has turned it into a hotel with a transatlantic theme, which is played out to most striking effect in the lobby, where a hull-like installation sweeps round to the restaurant (see p048). The bar, and top-floor Rumpus Room (T 3747 1026), are run by mixologist Ryan Chetiyawardana, aka Mr Lyan. Many of Platner's original fixtures, such as the brass door handles and lights, have been retained. Of the 359 rooms, the 43 accommodations (Loft Suite bedroom, above) with uninterrupted river views are the plum options. On the lower level, the Agua spa is open to non-guests. *20 Upper Ground, SE1, T 3747 1000, www.mondrianlondon.com*

The Beaumont

The masters of metropolitan dining, Chris Corbin and Jeremy King, have now turned their hand to the hotel business. Architects ReardonSmith and Richmond International transformed the 1926 building from a car park into opulent lodgings with art deco interiors. The real surprise is Room (above), a suite conceived by artist Antony Gormley that protrudes from the south wing like a Lego sentinel made of welded steel. The bedroom is lined with German oak and designed to immerse guests in a blackout. King's concept for the rest of the hotel was a bolthole for an imaginary ex-US army officer living it up in London in the Roaring Twenties. The best of the 73 rooms overlook Brown Heart Gardens, and the Colony Grill Room is the place to see and be seen. *Brown Hart Gardens, W1, T 7499 1001, www.thebeaumont.com*

24 HOURS

SEE THE BEST OF THE CITY IN JUST ONE DAY

Where to start, in a city that is as inscrutable and widely flung as it is packed with cultural highlights? The answer: don't attempt too much or travel too far. This day is about strolling, and the activities that London has never been better at: shopping, design and dining.

For ease of getting about, we concentrate on the centre of town. Dover Street Market (opposite) is much more than a shop – it is an introduction to the capital's creative landscape. It is also within walking distance of two of the city's finest green spaces. London's parks are its saving grace, and revivers for many a harried urbanite. Amble from Mayfair through Hyde Park and Kensington Gardens to reach the Serpentine Galleries (see p026) and dramatic Magazine restaurant, a delightful spot for lunch. We could suggest spending an entire day at the V&A (see p028), but for reasons of expediency we focus on the fashion gallery and its world-leading collection.

Come the evening, the dinner choices are vast and varied, but striking the balance between atmosphere and fabulous food is not always easy. That's why we have recommended The Palomar (see p031). You'll eat like a king, or a queen, and have fun doing so. It's not the place for a serene tête-à-tête, more a celebration of why London dining is so exciting right now. If you want to go East, start with drinks at Mission (see p034) and follow with a reservation at The Clove Club (see p042) or Lyle's (see p044).

For full addresses, see Resources.

11.00 Dover Street Market

Rei Kawakubo can be credited for leading the retail migration west of Bond Street and reinvigorating Mayfair. Mindful that the super-architect-designed luxury box was becoming a cliché, the Comme des Garçons creator opened Dover Street Market in a tired townhouse-turned-office building in 2004. She gutted the place and left the interior design to artists and set designers, such as Matt Moser-Clark and Gary Card. Kawakubo's idea, a series of artful installations for brands like Dior, Lanvin and her own Comme label, quickly hooked the fashion-forward. A decade on, it was time for a reinvention, in the spirit of DSM's beginnings. The jewellery area has been reimagined by Brit artist Tom Price, and the Rose Bakery café expanded.
17-18 Dover Street, W1, T 7518 0680, www.doverstreetmarket.com

12.30 Serpentine Galleries

Few London art spaces boast such lovely settings as these two galleries on either side of The Serpentine lake. The original venue occupies a 1930s tea room, and the newer one, the Sackler, is a former gunpowder store. Architect Zaha Hadid converted its vaulted brick interior in 2013, creating exhibition space and a futuristic extension (pictured) to house The Magazine restaurant (T 7298 7552).

Beneath its undulating white roof, chef Oliver Lange lends Japanese techniques to British ingredients. Serpentine's co-director, Julia Peyton-Jones, conceives a programme to do the site justice, notably the summer pavilion, designed each year by a major architect. Closed on Mondays. *Kensington Gardens/West Carriage Drive, W2, T 7402 6075, www.serpentinegalleries.org*

15.00 V&A fashion gallery
Architects 6a's refurbishment of the V&A's Octagon Court opened up one of the museum's grandest spaces. Built in 1909, the vast dome tops a series of arches and alcoves. A mezzanine was inserted in 1962 and this has been left in place, its impact reduced with slender white steel balustrades. The three large suspended light rings were added by 6a.
Cromwell Road, SW7, T 7942 2000

17.30 Curzon Victoria

Victoria is in the midst of an ambitious and rather messy regeneration, but there are pearls in the sea of scaffolding. As you walk down Victoria Street, look for Westminster City Hall (No 64), a 1966 International Style high-rise by Burnet, Tait and Partners. Steps away is the Curzon. Founded in 1934, the cinema chain blazed a trail, screening arthouse films in distinctive locations, including its original Mayfair home, in the basement of a 1966 modernist block, also by Burnet, Tait and Partners. The Victoria outpost is the first to be housed in a new structure, Lynch Architects' Zig Zag Building, and Afroditi Krassa's modish interiors offset light and dark beautifully. In all Curzons, look out for the Exhibition on Screen and director Q&A events.
58 Victoria Street, SW1, T 033 0500 1331, www.curzoncinemas.com

21.30 The Palomar

Tucked away in less well-trodden Soho, The Palomar is unique. Sibling owners Layo and Zoe Paskin once ran pioneering London DJ clubs The End and AKA, but their idea for a restaurant was born far away, in Jerusalem. After eating at the renowned Machneyuda, the Paskins kept in touch with its chefs, Yossi Elad, Assaf Granit and Uri Navon, and all eventually agreed to join forces in London. The Palomar launched in 2014, with Tomer Amedi in charge of the kitchen and a cuisine that fuses Arab, Jewish and Mediterranean influences. The mezze are moreish and there's a raw bar serving zesty dishes like fattoush. Christian Ducker's interior lends the place a casual glamour that suits the clientele to a tee. Reserve a table in the dining room or walk in and hope for a few free stools at the bar. *34 Rupert Street, W1, T 7439 8777*

URBAN LIFE

CAFÉS, RESTAURANTS, BARS AND NIGHTCLUBS

London weathers its fair share of fads, from Tiki clubs to converted Victorian loos, but there are just as many establishments making a mark by matching style and substance. Soho has its mojo back, and genuinely innovative venues such as Alan Yau's Duck and Rice (90 Berwick Street, W1) and The Palomar (see p031). If you're exploring Mayfair, Gymkhana (42 Albemarle Street, W1, T 3011 5900) is a must for Karam Sethi's Michelin-starred modern Indian cuisine.

Produce-led cooking is still high on the agenda, and in the New Wing of Somerset House, its doyenne, Skye Gyngell, has opened Spring (Lancaster Place, WC2, T 3011 0115). Blackfoot (46 Exmouth Market, EC1, T 7837 4384) is a porcine paradise, and the Gladwin brothers have boosted Chelsea dining with the rustic-chic Rabbit (172 King's Road, SW3, T 3750 0172). Londoners' passion for tapas is undiminished and Barrafina (10 Adelaide Street, WC2) has eased its walk-in queues with a branch in Covent Garden. Neither is the brasserie boom over; time will tell if the reborn Quaglino's (16 Bury Street, SW1, T 7930 6767) becomes the haunt it once was.

London's mixologists are in fine fettle, dreaming up cocktails made from locally brewed spirits and foraged herbs. Try Bourne & Hollingsworth Buildings (see p046) and seek out Mr Lyan. When he's not at the Mondrian (see p022), you'll find him at his own bar, the pioneering White Lyan (153-155 Hoxton Street, N1, T 3011 1153). *For full addresses, see Resources.*

Dabbous

When it launched in 2012, Ollie Dabbous' restaurant was a sensation. The power of Fay Maschler, the Pauline Kael of British food critics, and a Twitter frenzy, made securing a table an exercise in delayed gratification (it's only three months' wait these days). It didn't hurt that Dabbous looks like a rock star. His cooking, awarded a Michelin star, is still impressive, although the pressure is on to sustain the hype.

Many dishes are simple (tomato on toast), but the flavours are intense. The interior by Brinkworth is all bare-duct functionalism, with great attention to detail. If you're the impatient sort, snacks are served in the basement cocktail bar, Oskar's, helmed by co-owner Oskar Kinberg; or try the pair's lower-key Barnyard (T 7580 3842). *39 Whitfield Street, W1, T 7323 1544, www.dabbous.co.uk*

Mission
It didn't take Michael and Charlotte
Sager-Wilde long to exploit the success
of their first wine bar, Sager + Wilde
(T 8127 7330), opened in 2013. Their
second one, Mission, is tucked under
a railway arch, and done out with wood
panelling and a bronze bar. The palm
is a nod to the cellar, which centres on
California, like James de Jong's menu.
250 Paradise Row, E2, T 7613 0478

Curators Coffee Gallery

Like many of London's best coffee houses, Curators has Antipodean roots. Australians Catherine Seay and co-owners launched a café (T 7283 4642) near Leadenhall Market in 2012, which won over City workers. Now they've filled a caffeine gap just north of Oxford Circus. The two floors include a bright basement (above), which designers Jason Prain, Gus Thatcher and Ana-Foster Adams have handled with a light touch, using repurposed furnishings and hanging various artworks. Curators coffee is not cheap, but it is brewed with extreme care. Local roastery Nude Espresso supplies the house 'Exhibition' blend, a mix of beans from Brazil and El Salvador. The baristas have fun too, with 'Creations' combining ingredients like cascara and spices.
51 Margaret Street, W1, T 7580 2547, www.curatorscoffee.com

Lima Floral

When Peruvian food came to town a few years ago, some said it would be a passing trend. How wrong they were. Chef Virgilio Martinez, hugely respected for Central, his restaurant in Peru, opened Lima (T 3002 2640) in Fitzrovia in 2012, soon earning a Michelin star. Martinez has entrusted his second London kitchen to Robert Ortiz, whose cooking is a dream. This may be your first taste of maca root or *algarrobo* syrup, but you won't regret it. The flavours can be unusual but there isn't a wrong note on the menu; the beef *sudado* is sublime. B3's interiors offset wooden tables and white brick against electric blue and an abstract mural by Bluey Byrne (above). Downstairs in the *piqueos* bar, it's all about small plates and the house pisco cocktails. *14 Garrick Street, WC2, T 7240 5778, www.limafloral.com*

Story

Like policemen and chancellors, head chefs are getting younger. Tom Sellers is in his twenties but has already worked under Thomas Keller, René Redzepi and Tom Aikens. Indeed, the buzz surrounding Sellers meant his 2011 pop-up, Foreword, in Bethnal Green, was the hottest table in town. The foodie set salivated at the idea of his permanent restaurant, which arrived in 2013 on the site of an old Victorian toilet block, in a new wood-clad structure by Space Craft Architects, with interiors by Shoreditch firm Raven. Sellers' ambitious take on British cuisine is epitomised in dishes such as his beef-dripping candle (served with bread), and he offers only set menus, of six and 10 courses. Story's Michelin star may help soften that blow. *199 Tooley Street, SE1, T 7183 2117, www.restaurantstory.co.uk*

L'Anima

As one rather sharp reviewer pointed out, minimalism is neither easy nor cheap to pull off. It needs 'noble materials, precisely engineered'. At L'Anima, one of London's finest Italian restaurants, architect Claudio Silvestrin achieved an expensive minimalist aesthetic, orchestrating a space of cool drama with limestone floors and marble bathrooms. A glass partition separates the dining room from the bar (above), where the porphyry walls complement the white-leather seats. Chef Francesco Mazzei and his team cook impeccable, mostly southern Italian cuisine, and in 2014 opened a café (T 7422 7080) round the corner. Ideal for a breakfast meeting, or glass of prosecco, it also has a takeaway deli section selling artisanal Italian produce and wines.
1 Snowden Street, EC2, T 7422 7000, www.lanima.co.uk

Social Eating House

Jason Atherton has long outgrown the 'Gordon Ramsay acolyte' tag and steadily built up his own empire. This 2013 Soho restaurant was his third London opening, on the heels of Little Social (T 7870 3730), and was styled as a contemporary bistro by Russell Sage Studio. There's a Franco-speakeasy feel to the exposed-brick walls, whitewashed copper ceiling and pre-worn leather banquettes, amid which head chef Paul Hood serves high-class comfort food, such as ravioli of wild boar bolognaise. The first-floor bar (above), unofficially dubbed the Blind Pig, has a cocktail menu by Gareth Evans, ex of Pollen Street Social (T 7290 7600). In 2014, Atherton launched City Social (T 7877 7703), which has stellar views from its 24th-floor perch in Tower 42. *58 Poland Street, W1, T 7993 3251, www.socialeatinghouse.com*

The Clove Club

Launched in 2013, The Clove Club got London's food bloggerati all of a quiver. Indeed, cynical commentators suggested that the cooking was designed more to be Instagrammed than eaten. Isaac McHale's dishes are certainly beautiful, as is Owen Wall's tableware, but they also deliver taste-wise – the restaurant was given a Michelin star in 2014. The setting is the 1865 Shoreditch Town Hall, an Edwardian building that's slowly being converted into an arts complex. Working with architects Mango, the founders kept the interiors stark, with the open kitchen the centre of attention. Latterly of Upstairs at The Ten Bells (T 07530 492 986) in Spitalfields, McHale serves a seasonal British tasting menu, and set courses at lunch. For a simplified version of his creations, join the hip crowd at the bar ordering light bites. *Shoreditch Town Hall, 380 Old Street, EC1, T 7729 6496, www.thecloveclub.com*

Lyle's

Fergus Henderson has had a deep impact on modern British cuisine – and many an aspiring chef. James Lowe, the co-owner of Lyle's, spent years heading the kitchen at Henderson's St John Bread and Wine (see p052) and now runs his own restaurant, opened in 2014 with John Ogier. It's an airy dining room with a light-industrial elegance that has been brought about by B3, who tempered the coldness of the concrete with wooden furniture and tableware by local ceramicist Owen Wall. The dinner tasting menu (which caters for vegetarians and the allergy-afflicted) is built around British produce, which Lowe coaxes into complex, delicate creations as well as more robust dishes. This is cooking of the experimental sort, and we applaud that.

Tea Building, 56 Shoreditch High Street, E1, T 3011 5911, www.lyleslondon.com

Pizarro

As former executive chef of Brindisa in Borough Market, José Pizarro can make a legitimate claim to be the man who helped make Londoners tapas obsessives. We're not talking small plates; and certainly not foam or fluffed-up extractions. When he decided to go it alone, Pizarro moved to Bermondsey Street to open José (T 7403 4902), an authentic Spanish bar with tiles, barrels, terrific wines and sherries, and an unholy crush. He followed it with a larger, eponymous restaurant (above) down the road serving the same top-notch cuisine, but with the option of bigger portions. The locale is having a moment, and eateries and bars are filing in thick and fast. After your croquetas and chorizo, have a cocktail at Bermondsey Arts Club (T 7237 9552). *194 Bermondsey Street, SE1, T 7378 9455, www.josepizarro.com*

Bourne & Hollingsworth Buildings

Clerkenwell is brimming with designers and architects, who need to meet, greet, wine and dine – and in 2014 along came this cleverly arranged bar/restaurant, with nooks in which to work and play. The B&H team already had fans for its cocktail bars Bourne & Hollingsworth (T 7636 8228) and Reverend JW Simpson (T 3174 1155). This is a bigger enterprise, set in a 19th-century building converted by Box 9 and Red Deer.

More mod country house than urban-industrial, the whitewashed interior is charming. Gavin Weber created bespoke ironwork and the concrete bar (above), and Marcus Hazell made the tables, wicker chairs and handsome bar stools. Chef Alex Visciano needs to hit his stride, but you can expect a top tipple at the bar.
42 Northampton Road, EC1, T 3174 1156, www.bandhbuildings.com

Connaught Bar

Dating from 1897, the Connaught is the quintessential London luxury hotel. It promises and delivers discretion, and has a fierce resistance to novelty. However, it did benefit from a £70m overhaul in the noughties, which included a reimagining of the property's two bars. India Mahdavi redesigned the Coburg, and the late David Collins injected oodles of glamour to the Connaught (above), which has a separate entrance on Mount Street that is rather convenient if you've been on a shopping spree in Mayfair. A cocoon of marble, shimmering surfaces and black-leather banquettes, the interior, allied with a house martini, should ease the pain of any wallet-weakening endeavours. The Connaught Bar is closed on Sundays. *Carlos Place, W1, T 7314 3419, www.the-connaught.co.uk*

Sea Containers
The major appeal of this restaurant in the Mondrian (see p022) is its Thames-side setting on the South Bank. Seamus Mullen's globetrotting menu is based on a sharing concept. It spans small and large plates, and features produce from Borough Market. There's a raw bar and a wood grill; we highly recommend the creamy ricotta, and heritage pork chop.
20 Upper Ground, SE1, T 3747 1000

Library

At the Trafalgar Square end of St Martin's Lane, Library was set up in 2014 by Ronald Ndoro. As members' clubs go, this one gets our design vote. The interiors are by 19 Greek Street (see p070) and give the environment a cool, contemporary edge. There are vases by Tel Aviv's Noam Dover and Michal Cederbaum, and side tables by Beirut's Karen Chekerdjian; sustainable elements include surface materials made by Dian Simpson from recycled bottles, and furnishings repurposed by the charity Out of the Dark. Spread over several levels, Library encompasses a main room with mezzanine (above), a bar, a gym and six guest rooms. The restaurant, Kitchen, is open to the public for lunch, and bookings include a day pass to the club.
112 St Martin's Lane, WC2, T 3302 7912, www.lib-rary.com

Dock Kitchen

An elder statesman of British design, Tom Dixon has contributed to many fashionable bars and restaurants, and now a hotel, the Mondrian (see p022). He has also become a successful restaurateur. Conceived as a pop-up at Dixon's HQ back in 2009, in a converted Victorian building overlooking the Grand Union Canal, Dock Kitchen remained open and has thrived ever since. Stevie Parle, previously of The River Café

(T 7386 4200), is a former supper-clubber. Although fond of subcontinental cooking, the chef shuffles between countries and culinary styles as the mood takes him. Part of the Portobello Dock complex, the dining room is akin to a Dixon showroom with table service, but given his design nous, this is no bad thing at all.
342-344 Ladbroke Grove, W10,
T 8962 1610, www.dockkitchen.co.uk

St John Bread and Wine

Fergus Henderson and Trevor Gulliver opened Smithfield restaurant St John (T 7251 0848) in 1994. The British menu, by Henderson (an architect, who cooks with a modernist clarity of purpose), has a famed emphasis on offal and is puritan in its lack of elaboration. The venue itself certainly has a white-walled seriousness about it. The pair branched out in 2003 with St John Bread and Wine, which has a simplified menu and remains a first-class all-day restaurant – the smoked Gloucester Old Spot bacon sandwich is a fine way to start the morning. As the name suggests, this location is also part bakery and part wine shop. In 2014, the weekend-only St John Bakery (T 7237 5999) opened near foodie haunt Maltby Street Market.
94-96 Commercial Street, E1,
T 7251 0848, www.stjohngroup.uk.com

Polpo

Russell Norman and Richard Beatty's 2009 concept of a relocated *bàcaro* – a Venetian bar serving *cicheti*, the little dishes that are unique to the city – has been such a success that branches have since sprung up in Clerkenwell (T 7250 0034), Covent Garden (T 7836 8448) and Notting Hill (T 7229 3283). We like the original because it's located in an 18th-century townhouse that was once home to Canaletto, which makes the setting for savouring some *fritto misto* and Soave hard to beat. The no-reservation dinner policy can mean a queue, but you can wait at the bar if there's room. Norman designed the interior (bare bricks, tin ceiling, intimate tables), and has created the kind of relaxed and convivial ambience that keeps diners coming back. *41 Beak Street, W1, T 7734 4479, www.polpo.co.uk*

INSIDERS' GUIDE

ELIZA HIGGINBOTTOM AND YUNUS ASCOTT, DESIGNERS

Working from a studio in Fulham, Eliza Higginbottom and Yunus Ascott create distinctive jewellery that has graced film sets and catwalks (www.yunus-eliza.co.uk). For them, London is a constant inspiration. 'The wonderful architecture and gothic sculptures are full of stories – it's impossible not to discover something every day.'

In town for a meeting, they may have breakfast at a classic like Cecconi's (5a Burlington Gardens, W1, T 7434 1500), but when close to home, they adore Colombian eaterie Café Mambo (683 Fulham Road, SW6, T 7751 0380): 'A tiny joint with great music and *arepas*.' In Hatton Garden, the jewellery district, they'll grab coffee at hip café Prufrock (23-25 Leather Lane, EC1, T 7242 0467), and later on, if attending an event around Soho, some dumplings at the no-frills Jen Café (4-8 Newport Place, WC2). On a Thursday night, Gaz's Rockin' Blues at St Moritz (159 Wardour Street, W1) 'is a sure thing for dancing'. Over in Hoxton, The Bridge (15 Kingsland Road, E2, T 3489 2216) is a haunt for laidback drinks and a 'heady vibe'.

'Not for the squeamish', the Hunterian Museum (35-43 Lincoln's Inn Fields, WC2, T 7869 6560) is a rich source of ideas, as is the V&A (see p028) and the Wallace Collection (Manchester Square, W1, T 7563 9500). To get a totally different perspective on the city, they'll take the DLR to Trinity Buoy Wharf, and have a bite in the vintage diner car Fatboy's (64 Orchard Place, E14, T 7987 4334). *For full addresses, see Resources.*

ART AND DESIGN

GALLERIES, STUDIOS AND PUBLIC SPACES

At both the established and the experimental ends of the spectrum, London's reputation as a creative powerhouse cannot be disputed. Since the opening of Tate Modern (see p068) in 2000, the city, and its visitors, have displayed an insatiable appetite for contemporary visual culture. Radical modern galleries such as Whitechapel (see p059) and the ICA (12 Carlton House Terrace, SW1, T 7930 3647) paved the way decades earlier, of course, and influenced the type of art spaces that are now part of the fabric of the city.

The commercial scene is booming, and Mayfair's re-emergence as a focal point has seen the area draw, and in some cases draw back, art-dealer heavyweights. Victoria Miro (14 St George Street, W1, T 7336 8109) has returned here with her third London space, having launched on Cork Street in 1985, while Jules Wright's The Wapping Project (37 Dover Street, W1) has taken over the top floor of Ely House. In Soho, New York's Marian Goodman (5-8 Lower John Street, W1, T 7099 0089) has moved into a building converted by David Adjaye. Greenwich's Now Gallery (The Gateway Pavilions, SE10, T 3770 2212) is an intriguing take on architecture as artwork.

Designers such as Thomas Heatherwick and Barber & Osgerby have become national ambassadors, and London can now claim to match Paris in the clout of its design galleries. At the grass-roots level, young talent (see p065) is quietly pushing boundaries too. *For full addresses, see Resources.*

Street art

London has long been a hotbed of street art, and Shoreditch/Hoxton is one of its epicentres. It's here that Richard Howard-Griffin launched his eponymous gallery (T 7739 9970) in 2013, representing artists such as Thierry Noir and Pablo Delgado. Over in upmarket Fitzrovia, Lazarides (T 7636 5443) has been selling 'urban art' to affluent collectors for a while. Indeed, much of the genre is now commissioned rather than created covertly, and many a corporate firm has taken to using an eye-catching mural. One of our favourites is the *This Is The Place* lightbox installation (above) and attendant mural at Standard House (15 Bonhill Street, EC2), by graphic designers Craig & Karl. Located in London and NYC, the duo create brightly coloured pop illustrations, simple at first glance but more complex the longer you look.

Fourth Plinth

Dating to 1999, London's Fourth Plinth prize is funded by the mayor's office and run by the Arts Council, and is awarded to a different contemporary artist each year. The winning artwork is installed for 12 months or so on top of the empty plinth in Trafalgar Square, locus of the capital, and a gathering place for demonstrators, revellers and, famously, pigeons. When the 1845 square was designed by Charles Barry, the idea was to top the fourth plinth with a regal statue (like the other three), but lack of funds put paid to that. Today's civic adornments are different. Katharina Fritsch's big blue bird, *Hahn/Cock* (above), found a place in Londoners' hearts thanks to its uplifting colour and cheekiness. Next up, there will be interventions by Hans Haacke and British artist David Shrigley. *Trafalgar Square, WC2, www.london.gov.uk*

Whitechapel Gallery

Occupying an Arts and Crafts building by Charles Harrison Townsend, Whitechapel Gallery was launched to bring art to the local community, and has endured as one of London's most dynamic art institutions. Since its founding in 1901, it has punched far above its weight. It was the only British gallery to exhibit Picasso's *Guernica* in 1939 (reinterpreted by Goshka Macuga, above), and held career-defining shows for then-emerging artists Bridget Riley, Richard Hamilton, David Hockney and Gilbert & George. It was expanded in the noughties, taking over the library next door, with the new sections conceived by Witherford Watson Mann and Robbrecht en Daem. Local artist Rachel Whiteread created *Tree of Life* for the facade.
77-82 Whitechapel High Street, E1,
T 7522 7888, www.whitechapelgallery.org

Carpenters Workshop Gallery

Over the past decade, Frenchmen Loïc Le Gaillard and Julien Lombrail have been participating gallerists in the 'is it art/is it design?' debate. Since they launched in an old carpenter's workshop in Chelsea, in 2006, they've shown the type of conceptual works that blur the boundaries between the disciplines. They relocated to Albemarle Street in 2008 and, as an edgier kind of gallery in a then rather staid Mayfair, Carpenters did a lot to nudge the area in a more contemporary direction. The designers they have exhibited include Studio Job, Johanna Grawunder ('No Whining on the Yacht', pictured), Random International and Rick Owens, all now members of the design aristocracy. Carpenters continues to pursue the cutting edge, on the hunt for fresh interpretations of art/design. *3 Albemarle Street, W1, T 3051 5939, www.carpentersworkshopgallery.com*

Isokon Building and Gallery

This 1934 block of flats was the radical vision of architect Wells Coates, and Jack and Molly Pritchard of design company Isokon. The minimal, space-efficient units, featuring new materials, drew the prime movers of the modern movement. Walter Gropius and his wife, Ise, occupied flat 15; Marcel Breuer lived here; and the in-house Isobar was frequented by Henry Moore and Barbara Hepworth. In the noughties, the reinforced-concrete structure and interiors were meticulously restored by Avanti Architects, and the garage now houses a gallery, curated by Skandium co-founder Magnus Englund, charting the building's history. Isokon's pioneering plywood furniture (opposite) and some fascinating ephemera are on display. Open weekends, March to October. *Lawn Road, NW3, www.isokongallery.co.uk*

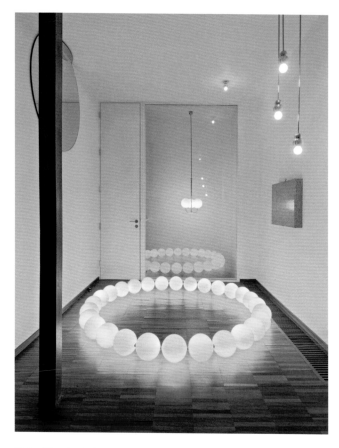

Michael Anastassiades

Lower Marsh is a short street lined with old-fashioned retailers and hip newcomers, minutes from Waterloo Station. Michael Anastassiades moved here in 1999, and his studio stands out like a jewel box amid the other shopfronts. Anastassiades and architect Wim de Mul gutted the house that now serves as the designer's live-work space and gallery, for the minimal, highly abstracted pieces in marble, brass and glass that have gained him a global following. His first mass-production contract was with the Italian company Flos, for whom he designs lighting such as 'Ama' (above), made of mouth-blown opaline glass and brass. It was inspired by Japan's female pearl-divers, and the piece was a standout of LDF 2014.
22 Lower Marsh, SE1, T 7928 7527, www.michaelanastassiades.com

James Shaw

Like most designers of his generation, RCA graduate James Shaw sees sustainability as integral to his work. The setting for his current studio, South-East London's brutalist Aylesbury Estate, is appropriate, as the housing complex, built from 1963 to 1977, is undergoing part-demolition and part-regeneration. Shaw also focuses on renewability. His 'Well Proven Chair' was a collaboration with Marjan van Aubel, on show at LDF 2013. Drawn to the idea of repurposing industrial waste, the pair experimented mixing sawdust with bio-resin to create a new material. Recently, Shaw has designed with eco-friendly linoleum. The 'Crazy Marm' coffee table (above) has a concrete base covered in salvaged lino, whose elaborate pattern is offset by the piece's simple form. *www.jamesmichaelshaw.co.uk*

David Gill Galleries
A hugely influential figure on the design scene since 1987, David Gill has helped the careers of Marc Newson and Ron Arad, among others, and commissioned Zaha Hadid's foray into furniture in 2007. His airy St James's gallery specialises in works that are future collectables. Mattia Bonetti and Barnaby Barford showed new pieces in 'Chandeliers' (pictured).
2-4 King Street, SW1, T 3051 5939

Tate Modern

When Herzog & de Meuron created a sister venue to Tate Britain (T 7887 8888) in an old power station in South-East London, it seemed like madness. Now Tate Modern is a blueprint for the capital's modern art museums. The architecture is as much of an allure as the art, and the rawness of Sir Giles Gilbert Scott's building remains potent. There's a stark industrial beauty to the cathedral-like turbine hall, which can accommodate vast installations such as Richard Tuttle's *I Don't Know. The Weave of Textile Language* (above). In 2016, Herzog & de Meuron's extension, a sharply angled structure with a perforated-brick facade, will add three gallery floors. Along with the underground Tanks, the former oil cylinders, the new exhibition space will allow for a more diverse programme. *Bankside, SE1, T 7887 8888, www.tate.org.uk*

The Photographers' Gallery

Host of the prestigious Deutsche Börse prize for contemporary photography, this was the world's first independent gallery devoted to the medium. Founded in 1971 by Sue Davies, in a former Lyons tea bar in Soho, it gave Juergen Teller, Andreas Gursky and Taryn Simon their first British shows. Outgrowing the original site, the gallery moved to a former warehouse on Ramillies Street in 2008 and, two years later, embarked on a redesign by Irish architects O'Donnell + Tuomey (see p077). The revamped interior, unveiled two years later, has three levels of exhibition space, a digital 'Media Wall', presenting work by a rota of artists (Susan Sloan, above), a camera obscura (check for opening times), café, bookshop and print sales room.
16-18 Ramillies Street, W1, T 7087 9300, www.thephotographersgallery.org.uk

MASTERPIECE

Analogia Project
Hamajima Takuya
Valentin Lolleman
Rasmus Baekkel fex
Tomas Libertiny
Studio deFORM

19 Greek Street

Set across a Soho townhouse, 19 Greek Street proves that sustainable design does not have to mean a sacrifice of style. Its founder, Marc Péridis, gathers together collections that focus on innovation and the most accomplished examples of green design. Some of the early pieces dating to the gallery's 2012 launch are still on display, such as the 'Re-imagined' series of upcycled chairs by Nina Tolstrup. Recent works have included Rasmus Baekkel Fex's 'Father & Son' chair, Valentin Loellmann's 'Madame' wardrobe (both above) from his MS & MME project, and Dirk Vander Kooij's 'Melting Pot' table, made of waste material from 3D printing. A curator with a social conscience, Péridis is planning a charity, 16. Visits are by appointment.
19 Greek Street, W1, T 7734 5594, www.19greekstreet.com

White Cube

Jay Jopling launched White Cube in 1993. The Mayfair building (T 7930 5373) was only 20.5 sq m but quickly became the city's most exciting art space, helping to kickstart the Brit Art phenomenon. The 2000 follow-up in Hoxton announced the East as a rallying point for contemporary art. At 5,400 sq m, Jopling's third London gallery (above) has the size and ambition of a public establishment, with museum-quality exhibitions, an auditorium and a bookshop. Three large spaces show artists that are represented by White Cube, and three smaller areas provide a platform for younger, emerging talent. The 1970s brick warehouse was converted by architects Casper Mueller Kneer, whose adaptation of the front canopy is a nod to Ed Ruscha. *144-152 Bermondsey Street, SE1, T 7930 5373, www.whitecube.com*

ARCHITOUR

A GUIDE TO LONDON'S ICONIC BUILDINGS

While the threat of London becoming 'Dubai on Thames' (more than 200 towers are said to be on the drawing board) is the issue grabbing headlines, the capital's modernist legacy remains one of its architectural treats. Nowhere can remove you so totally from the mess of histories that make up the city as the Barbican (see p078). Stroll along its elevated walkways and you'll feel as if you are in a retro futurescape. The 1934 Isokon Building (see p062) in bucolic Belsize Park is a flashback to the beginnings of modernist London, which perhaps reached its zenith in Denys Lasdun's 1958 Royal College of Physicians (11 St Andrews Place, N1). Another classic of the era, the 1962 Commonwealth Institute (Kensington High Street, W8), designed by Robert Matthew, Johnson-Marshall & Partners, is undergoing renovation to turn it into a new home for the Design Museum (28 Shad Thames, SE1, T 7403 6933). John Pawson is handling the interiors, and OMA and Arup are tackling the exterior, including the distinctive copper-clad roof.

The regeneration of King's Cross dwarfs even the ambition of the Barbican. John McAslan's station concourse (see p074) is the clearest demonstration yet of how attractive this district of the city could be, while the London School of Economics' Saw Swee Hock Student Centre (see p077) is a shining example of how imaginative architecture can enliven the smallest of urban plots.

For full addresses, see Resources.

New Court

OMA's home for Rothschild was the firm's first London project, and in the City's tight confines it makes most of its neighbours look lumpen and ill conceived. A 10-storey mesh cube topped by a 'sky pavilion', it displays a lightness of touch that's missing from Foster + Partners' The Walbrook, the partly occupied squat metal blob that it overlooks. Nathan Mayer Rothschild first moved to the St Swithin's Lane site in 1809. This fourth headquarters of the family business, now a financial advisory company, opened its doors at the end of 2011. Given that the entrance is on a skinny medieval cut-through, it's hard to take in the facade at street level. What you do get is a marble forecourt and, for the first time in 200 years, views through to Christopher Wren's St Stephen Walbrook church.

St Swithin's Lane, EC4

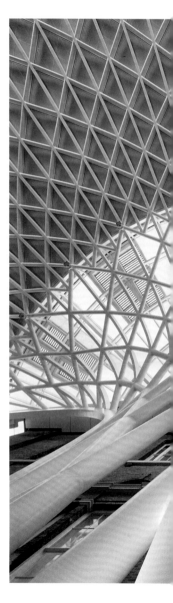

King's Cross Western Concourse

Thanks to the relocations of *The Guardian* newspaper and Central Saint Martins arts college, the area north of King's Cross station is emerging as the happening new quarter that has long been promised (even if a good deal of its 27 hectares of brownfield is still to be developed). Like the nearby Granary Square, the terminus itself has come to feel like an integral part of a lively new 'hood. From outside, the Western Concourse resembles a flying saucer that has crashed into the Victorian hulk of the 1852 station. Inside, it is a giant open dome with a span of 52m. It is supported by a cluster of steel stalks, ascending 20m into the air, which sprout a latticework of branches that arc back to the ground. Inevitably, there are lots of shops and eateries, but the enclosed plaza appears less like an upmarket mall than neighbouring St Pancras does.
Euston Road/York Way, N1

National Theatre

This is the most visible example of heroic modernism in London, as if its architect Denys Lasdun sought to make landscapes out of buildings. The design had to include three theatres and all sorts of backstage areas, as well as cafés, bars and foyers, yet it remains one of the most dramatic to grace the Thames. The interior spaces, the largest being the Olivier Theatre, were conceived to be just as impressive.

A renovation has led to some significant changes, including a revamp of the smaller Cottesloe Theatre, which reopened as the Dorfman in 2014, and a new high-level walkway that affords a peek into backstage workshops. It has also created more public space, and eating and drinking options, like the restaurant House (T 7452 3600). *South Bank, SE1, T 7452 3400, www.nationaltheatre.org.uk*

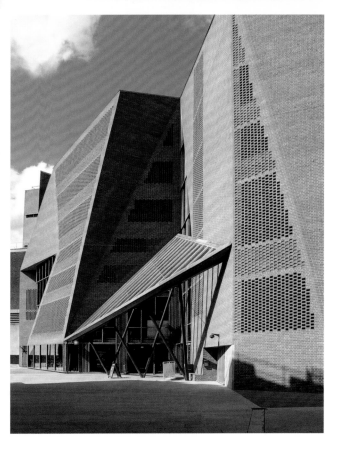

Saw Swee Hock Student Centre (SAW)

O'Donnell + Tuomey's 2014 addition to the LSE is joyously dynamic – it's as if the narrow streets surrounding it are clasping the energetic structure in their grip. The uniqueness of the building stems from its unorthodox shape and perforated red-brick facade, which slopes outwards and skywards at varying angles; the geometry's sharpness is tempered by Jatoba-wood window frames. Beyond the canopied entrance, the interior was conceived to underscore the theme of movement, and a wide staircase spirals through the central space. The exploitation of natural light and ventilation earned SAW the highest BREEAM credentials, to add to its many other awards, including the 2014 RIBA London Building of the Year. *1 Sheffield Street, WC2, T 7405 7686, www.lse.ac.uk*

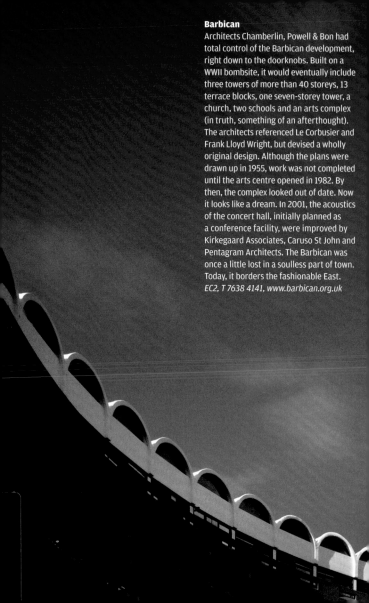

Barbican

Architects Chamberlin, Powell & Bon had total control of the Barbican development, right down to the doorknobs. Built on a WWII bombsite, it would eventually include three towers of more than 40 storeys, 13 terrace blocks, one seven-storey tower, a church, two schools and an arts complex (in truth, something of an afterthought). The architects referenced Le Corbusier and Frank Lloyd Wright, but devised a wholly original design. Although the plans were drawn up in 1955, work was not completed until the arts centre opened in 1982. By then, the complex looked out of date. Now it looks like a dream. In 2001, the acoustics of the concert hall, initially planned as a conference facility, were improved by Kirkegaard Associates, Caruso St John and Pentagram Architects. The Barbican was once a little lost in a soulless part of town. Today, it borders the fashionable East. *EC2, T 7638 4141, www.barbican.org.uk*

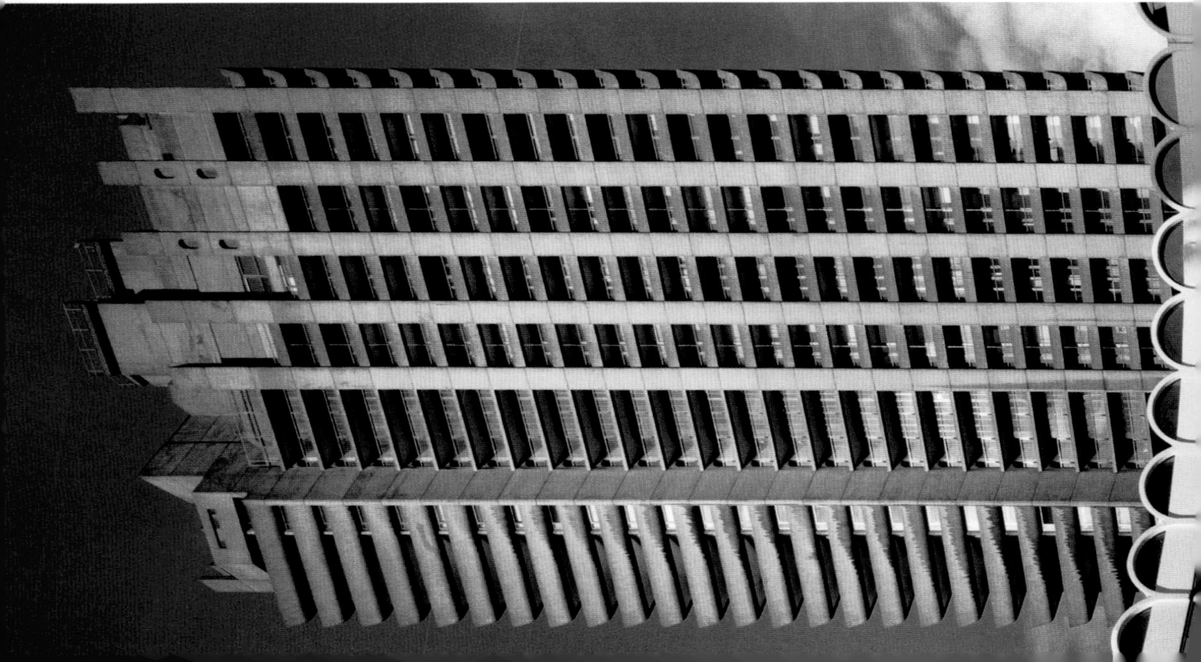

SHOPS

THE BEST RETAIL THERAPY AND WHAT TO BUY

This city boasts some of the most rewarding and diverse shopping you'll find, from innovative department store Liberty (see p095) to new-wave lifestyle emporium The Goodhood Store (see p084). In the centre, Mayfair may be predictable but it's bountiful, and has the exciting Dover Street Market (see p025) and Paul Smith (see p086). Mount Street continues to strengthen as a luxury retail strip, and Roksanda Ilincic (No 9, W1, T 7613 6499) has made her standalone debut here, in a store designed by David Adjaye. In evolving Holborn, independent shops, like Darkroom (see p088), thrive on Lamb's Conduit Street thanks to a principled landlord.

Shoreditch teems with hip retailers in the vein of O'Dell's (see p082), and Redchurch Street is a chief thoroughfare. Check out Hostem (No 41-43, E2, T 7739 9733), which sells clothes for men and women, and the interesting product designs at Monologue (No 93, E2, T 7729 0400). Close by, there is more design to peruse at Jasper Morrison (see p090), Gallery Fumi (opposite) and Made in Ratio (16 Holywell Row, EC2, T 7247 3414), the showroom for Brodie Neill's furniture. West London lacks the edginess of the East, but there are a number of bright spots. Mint (see p085) is an important resource for interiors, and newcomer Native & Co (116 Kensington Park Road, W11, T 7243 0418) sells crafts selected by Sharon Jo-Yun Hung and Chris Yoshiro Green.

For full addresses, see Resources.

Gallery Fumi

Since 2008, when it was set up by Valerio Capo and Sam Pratt in Shoreditch, Fumi has exerted an important influence on the city's design community. Now situated in a large, light-filled Hoxton space, it sells unique and limited-edition pieces, some of which the gallery commissions. Alongside foreign designers, such as Paris-based glassblower Jeremy Maxwell Wintrebert and Amsterdam's Studio Markunpoika,

London makers are well represented. Max Lamb, who has an international reputation, makes furniture and objects often inspired by his native Cornwall, while Sam Orlando Miller's work has a sculptural dimension. Fumi also hosts exhibitions and is a fixture on the design-fair circuit. Visits are by appointment. *2nd floor, 16 Hoxton Square, N1, T 7490 2366, www.galleryfumi.com*

O'Dell's

Tom O'Dell's small, whitewashed store, once a Jewish bakery owned by the family of British artist Leon Kossoff, reveals his keen eye for artisanal wares. The original tiled floor has been renovated but the rest of the interior stripped back to show off its new goods. O'Dell worked for Nigel Hall before setting up on his own in 2014. His aim was to stick to menswear, but he's broadened the range to accessories and homewares. Many products are exclusives and there is a deliberate focus on British makers. Among them, Rachel Scott is an RCA-trained painter-turned-weaver from Pimlico who makes rugs with geometric patterns; and Yorkshire's Turner & Harper craft products such as this walnut and hog-bristle banister brush (above), £40. *24 Calvert Avenue, E2, T 3012 9416, www.odellsstore.com*

The Goodhood Store

Jo Sindle and Kyle Stewart's boutique is the epitome of modern-day Shoreditch. Launched back in 2007, it has outgrown its alternative image to become establishment cool. Grown-up Goodhood is a purveyor of sleek luxury casualwear, and design-led home accessories by the likes of Hay and Studio Arhoj. Divided across two levels, the interior incorporates elements from the old shop, such as the lightbox that became a Goodhood emblem, and has display installations used for pop-up events. On the lower level, the Commune café is run by Brett Redman of Elliot's in Borough Market. As well as having a sharp eye for über-cool European brands, the owners have a penchant for Japanese labels, such as Tokyo's Neighbourhood and FPAR. *151 Curtain Road, EC2, T 7729 3600, www.goodhoodstore.com*

Mint

Established by Lina Kanafani in 1998, Mint remains a leading light of West London retail, with a reputation for design that goes beyond the usual suspects. Occupying a two-level space off Brompton Road, the store commissions limited-edition and one-off pieces that often demonstrate the owner's fearlessness and aversion to the safety of quiet good taste. Many products have been selected for their playful use of materials and unorthodox approach to craft techniques; the 'Bon Bon' side table is cast from layers of resin to resemble an edible sweet, and the art deco-inspired 'No Screw No Glue' desk and chair consist solely of interlocked pieces of laser-cut steel. You'll also come across a covetable selection of handcrafted home accessories. *2 North Terrace, SW3, T 7225 2228, www.mintshop.co.uk*

Paul Smith

An inveterate traveller, Paul Smith has always been a collector of antiques and mementos. In the noughties, he put a lot of his trove into his furniture and curiosities shop, housed in a Georgian townhouse in Mayfair. In 2013, the store was enlarged and renovated to create a new flagship for Smith's fashion and assemblage of objets, art and furniture. Beyond the modernist chairs reupholstered in Paul Smith fabric, there's a women's shoe room decked out with dominoes, and a menswear space anchored by Benchmark furniture. What draws you in first, though, is the exterior, designed with architects 6a. Laid on top of black brick, the intricate cast-iron frontage has a pattern of overlapping circles and Smith's drawings imprinted in the panels. *9 Albemarle Street, W1, T 7493 4565, www.paulsmith.co.uk*

Darkroom

In 2009, Rhonda Drakeford and Lulu Roper-Caldbeck opened this compact concept store to sell unique homewares and accessories from across the globe. The pair also stock their own designs, and astute collaborations, such as the unisex sunglasses made with British company Larke. Design team Frank created the furniture for the interior.
52 Lamb's Conduit Street, WC1, T 7831 7244

Jasper Morrison Shop

The work of celebrated British designer Jasper Morrison has a broad span, from tableware and furniture, to a tram and a bus stop. In 2006, together with Naoto Fukasawa, he put together an exhibition entitled 'Super Normal', whose theme became a manifesto. Reacting against overelaborate design, and contemporaries becoming overexcited at being told they were 'artists', Morrison held steady with his dedication to 'the shape of everyday things'. For a recent kitchen range, which includes the 'Palma' kettle (above), £165, he collaborated with artisanal Japanese company Oigen. In Morrison's shop, tucked inside his Shoreditch studio, expect plenty more examples of the simple and the elegantly practical. Closed weekends.
24b Kingsland Road, E2,
www.jaspermorrisonshop.com

Tracey Neuls

Shoes that can withstand the harsh city streets, in all weathers, and look good, are rare. Enter Tracey Neuls, a London designer whose approach marries flair and function. Shortlisted for a 2014 award by the Design Museum (see p072), Neuls' 'Bike' line is chic and cycle-friendly. The shoes, which come in various styles for women and men, including the 'George' boot (above), £195, are produced using vegetable-dyed leather, and have rubber soles and a reflective strip at the back. Neuls' Marylebone store is known for its innovative displays, and she also has a branch in Shoreditch (T 7018 0872). Team your treads with high-vis clothing from Henrichs (www.henrichs.co.uk), and you'll never look better on your bike.

29 Marylebone Lane, W1, T 7935 0039, www.traceyneuls.com

Margaret Howell

A stalwart of British fashion, Margaret Howell graduated in the late 1960s from Goldsmiths College. She began producing men's shirts in the 1970s, wholesaling to future fashion giants Ralph Lauren and Paul Smith. In 1977, in collaboration with Joseph's Joseph Ettedgui, she opened a store on South Molton Street. In the past decade, Howell has enjoyed a renaissance as a champion of immaculately tailored casualwear for men and women, with an emphasis on natural materials such as cotton, linen and tweed, and subtle dyes and colours. Her Wigmore Street flagship, designed by William Russell of Pentagram, also displays British modernist furniture, crafts and sometimes art. She's produced many reissues in collaboration with Ercol, Anglepoise and Robert Welch, as well as a take on Ernest Race's 1955 'Heron' chair. *34 Wigmore Street, W1, T 7009 9009, www.margarethowell.co.uk*

Alexander McQueen

The late Alexander McQueen's Savile Row apprenticeship was central to his story, informing the sharp tailoring that defined the designer's work, so it's fitting that the label opened a flagship menswear store here – an ambition of McQueen's. The space, though, is more airy gallery than dark *salon privé*. It even has a large glass vitrine to hold artworks curated by Sadie Coles, whose HQ is nearby (T 7493 8611).

Creative director Sarah Burton worked with David Collins on the design, which conveys a wit that McQueen would have enjoyed. The shop also offers a tailoring service. The McQ line is sold in a Dover Street store (T 7318 2220), another Collins collaboration, and there's also a showroom located on Old Bond Street (T 7355 0088). *9 Savile Row, W1, T 7494 8840, www.alexandermcqueen.com*

Liberty

Renowned for its trademark prints, this affectionately regarded shop has long been synonymous with luxury and international design. The store was opened in 1875 by Arthur Liberty, who did not want 'to follow existing fashions, but to create new ones'. It subsequently stocked objets d'art and homewares from North Africa, Japan and the East. The Tudor-style building, by Edwin T Hall and his son Edwin S Hall, was constructed in 1924 from the timbers of two ships. In the past decade, following a strategic tune-up, Liberty has become a progressive emporium selling clothes, furnishings and much more. The focused buying skills of the fashion team are more akin to a sharp-minded independent than a label-bagging department store.
210-220 Regent Street, W1, T 7734 1234, www.liberty.co.uk

ESCAPES

WHERE TO GO IF YOU WANT TO LEAVE TOWN

London has no Hamptons or Sitges, although the Cotswolds and New Forest are weekend getaways with gourmet pubs and country retreats. There's the modish Cowley Manor (T 01242 870 900) near Cheltenham, while Lime Wood (Beaulieu Road, Lyndhurst, T 02380 287 167) in Hampshire has interiors by David Collins and a Martin Brudnizki-designed restaurant run by Angela Hartnett and Luke Holder. In nearby Brockenhurst, The Pig (Beaulieu Road, T 01590 622 354) is renowned for its cooking and has a coastal sibling in Studland, The Pig on the Beach (Manor Road, T 01929 450 288). Bray, in Berkshire, is a village bristling with Michelin stars, thanks to Heston Blumenthal's The Fat Duck (T 01628 580 333) and Alain Roux's The Waterside Inn (Ferry Road, T 01628 620 691).

On the art trail, Albion Barn (Church Hill, Little Milton, T 01844 277 960; by appointment) in Oxfordshire is a farm-turned-gallery that exhibits both artists and designers. In 2014, Hauser & Wirth made the Somerset town of Bruton a cultural draw, opening an art complex (opposite), as well as Roth Bar & Grill (T 01749 814 700), run by local inn At The Chapel (28 High Street, T 01749 814 070). Cross-country, Margate is the location of the Turner Contemporary (see p102). For architourists, there are fine examples of modernism close to London, including De La Warr Pavilion (see p100) and The Homewood (Portsmouth Road, Esher, T 01372 476 424).
For full addresses, see Resources.

Hauser & Wirth Somerset

One of London's largest commercial art spaces, Hauser & Wirth's gallery in Savile Row (T 7287 2300) is a reworking of an Eric Parry edifice by American architect Annabelle Selldorf. Now it boasts a rural counterpoint. Spread across a collection of 18th-century buildings on Durslade Farm, H&W Somerset is gallery, education centre, guesthouse and restaurant, all in one. Benjamin + Beauchamp restored the original architecture, adding two wings, and Laplace handled the interiors. Piet Oudolf's landscaping serves as a sculpture park for larger works (Thomas Houseago, *Large Lamp I*; Subodh Gupta, *Untitled*, overleaf). Manuela and Iwan Wirth are locals, and they have pushed community engagement to the fore. Closed Mondays. *Dropping Lane, Bruton, T 01749 814 060, www.hauserwirthsomerset.com*

De La Warr Pavilion, Bexhill-on-Sea

Completed in 1935, Erich Mendelsohn and Serge Chermayeff's De La Warr Pavilion, situated on the East Sussex coast, was the country's first modernist public building. The open competition to design a seaside entertainment complex happened to be announced within a couple of months of Mendelsohn arriving in England in 1933, and the German émigré, who was already a renowned figure in European architecture, hit the project at some speed. He created an impossibly glamorous docked-liner of a structure, with large glass windows and curving terraces, and a central, swirling chrome-and-steel staircase (opposite). An £8m restoration by architects John McAslan + Partners helped re-establish the pavilion as one of southern England's most important cultural buildings.
Marina, T 01424 229 111, www.dlwp.com

Turner Contemporary, Margate

A faded seaside town in Kent, Margate is probably now best known for its part in Tracey Emin's open wound of a life story. 'Whatever I do, part of Margate always comes with me,' she said. It seems right, then, that an art gallery is being viewed as a lever for the town's reversal of terminal decline. The Turner Contemporary, which was designed by David Chipperfield and opened in 2011, is named after Margate's other artist-in-residence, JMW Turner, who went to school here and returned often, because he loved the light (and a local hotel keeper). Chipperfield's building, a series of elegant, angular art sheds, is built on the site of the guesthouse where Turner painted, and is a delight because of the way it plays with light on the inside. *Rendezvous, T 01843 233 000, www.turnercontemporary.org*

NOTES
SKETCHES AND MEMOS

RESOURCES
CITY GUIDE DIRECTORY

HOTELS
ADDRESSES AND ROOM RATES

Ace Hotel 017
Room rates:
double, from £500;
deluxe, from £520;
suite, from £950
100 Shoreditch High Street, E1
T 7613 9800
www.acehotel.com/london

At the Chapel 096
Room rates:
double, from £150
28 High Street
Bruton
Somerset
T 01749 814 070
www.atthechapel.co.uk

The Beaumont 023
Room rates:
double, from £395;
Room, from £2,250
Brown Hart Gardens, W1
T 7499 1001
www.thebeaumont.com

Chiltern Firehouse 016
Room rates:
double, from £780
1 Chiltern Street, W1
T 7073 7653
www.chilternfirehouse.com

Citizen M 016
Room rates:
double, from £100
20 Lavington Street, SE1
T 3519 1680
www.citizenm.com

Claridge's 016
Room rates:
double, from £450
Brook Street, W1
T 7629 8860
www.claridges.co.uk

Cowley Manor 096
Room rates:
double, from £295
Cowley
Gloucestershire
T 01242 870 900
www.cowleymanor.com

The Dorchester 016
Room rates:
double, from £675
Park Lane, W1
T 7629 8888
www.thedorchester.com

The Edition 021
Room rates:
double, from £295;
Loft, from £535
10 Berners Street, W1
T 7781 0000
www.editionhotels.com

Ham Yard Hotel 020
Room rates:
double, from £375
1 Ham Yard, W1
T 3642 2000
www.firmdalehotels.com

The Hoxton Holborn 016
Room rates:
double, from £70
199-206 High Holborn, WC1
T 7661 3000
www.thehoxton.com

Lime Wood 096
Room rates:
double, from £255
Beaulieu Road
Lyndhurst
Hampshire
T 02380 287 167
www.limewoodhotel.co.uk

Mondrian 022
Room rates:
double, from £235;
Loft Suite, from £500
20 Upper Ground, SE1
T 3747 1000
www.mondrianlondon.com

The Pig 096
Room rates:
double, from £140
Beaulieu Road
Brockenhurst
Hampshire
T 01590 622 354
www.thepighotel.com

The Pig on the Beach 096
Room rates:
double, from £120
Manor Road
Studland
Dorset
T 01929 450 288
www.thepighotel.com

Qbic 016
Room rates:
double, from £70
42 Adler Street, E1
T 3021 3300
www.qbichotels.com

Rosewood 018
Room rates:
double, £590;
Grand Premier Suite 227, £750
252 High Holborn, WC1
T 7781 8888
www.rosewoodhotels.com

The Savoy 016
Room rates:
double, from £395
Strand, WC2
T 7836 4343
www.fairmont.com/savoy

Town Hall Hotel 016
Room rates:
double, from £330
Patriot Square, E2
T 7871 0460
www.townhallhotel.com

Zetter Townhouse 016
Room rates:
prices on request
28-30 Seymour Street, W1
T 7324 4567
www.thezetter.com

WALLPAPER* CITY GUIDES

Executive Editor
Jeremy Case

Author
Rachael Moloney

Art Editor
Eriko Shimazaki

Photography Editor
Elisa Merlo
Assistant Photography Editor
Nabil Butt

Editorial Assistant
Emilee Jane Tombs

Contributor
Nick Compton

Sub-Editor
Nick Mee

Production Controller
Sophie Kullmann

Original Design
Loran Stosskopf
Map Illustrator
Russell Bell

Wallpaper* ® is a
registered trademark
of IPC Media Limited

First published 2006
Revised and updated
2008, 2009, 2011 and 2013
Eighth edition 2015

© Phaidon Press Limited

All prices and venue
information are correct at
time of going to press,
but are subject to change.

Contacts
wcg@phaidon.com
@wallpaperguides

More City Guides
www.phaidon.com/travel

Phaidon Press Limited
Regent's Wharf
All Saints Street
London N1 9PA

Phaidon Press Inc
65 Bleecker Street
New York, NY 10012

Phaidon® is a registered
trademark of Phaidon
Press Limited

www.phaidon.com

A CIP Catalogue record for
this book is available from
the British Library.

Printed in China

ISBN 978 0 7148 6849 3

PHOTOGRAPHERS

LONDON
A COLOUR-CODED GUIDE TO THE HOT 'HOODS

CENTRAL
Fitzrovia and Holborn have more of a buzz these days, and Soho is happening again

NORTH
King's Cross is still arriving as an anchor district, but has already been transformed

THE CITY
The cranes and high-rises keep on coming, and so do more exciting nightlife options

SOUTH-WEST
If you want to snare a royal, start here. But search out the area's cultural highlights too

WEST
Stucco central, this is what first-time visitors expect to find everywhere in the city, sadly

WESTMINSTER
After a glimpse of the urban gothic, explore St James's and galleries such as the ICA

EAST
Shoreditch remains a hangout, but the hipsters continue to shift ever eastwards

SOUTH-EAST
One of the fastest-changing areas of London is heading upwards at a dizzying rate

For a full description of each neighbourhood, see the Introduction.
Featured venues are colour-coded, according to the district in which they are located.